C000262405

contents

2–3   flavour hits

4–31   recipes

32–33   prawn pick-me-ups

34–59   recipes

60–61   glossary

62   index

63   facts & figures

British & North American Readers
Please note that Australian cup and spoon
measurements are metric. A quick conversion
guide appears on page 63.

flavour hits

*A plain piece of fish turns into a mouth-watering meal with the addition
of a hit of flavour. Each recipe on this spread can be served over
four pan-fried or barbecued whole fish, or fish fillets, cutlets or steaks.*

dill and caper dressing
Combine 2 tablespoons drained baby capers,
1 tablespoon finely chopped fresh dill, 1 teaspoon
grated lemon rind and 1/3 cup lemon juice.
serves 4
per serving 0.1g fat; 36kJ (9 cal)

olive paste
Blend or process 200g seeded black olives, 1/4 cup
drained capers, 1/3 cup each of fresh dill and fresh
parsley, 2 garlic cloves and 2 tablespoons lemon juic
serves 4
per serving 0.6g fat; 253kJ (60 cal)

anchovy butter
Combine 100g soft butter, 6 drained chopped
anchovy fillets, 1 crushed garlic clove and
1 tablespoon chopped fresh basil in small bowl.
Spoon mixture onto piece of foil, shape into log; roll
up firmly. Refrigerate until firm; cut slices and serve.
serves 4
per serving 21.1g fat; 812kJ (194 cal)

chilli lime dressing
Combine 2 tablespoons each of lime juice and brov
sugar, 1 tablespoon each of rice wine and fish sauc
1/2 teaspoon each of sesame oil and grated fresh gi
1 crushed garlic clove and 2 teaspoons sweet chilli s
serves 4
per serving 0.7g fat; 180kJ (43 cal)

walnut gremolata
Combine ⅓ cup finely chopped toasted walnuts,
2 tablespoons chopped lemon rind, ¼ cup chopped
fresh parsley and 1 crushed garlic clove.
serves 4
per serving 7g fat; 296kJ (71 cal)

tomato and coriander salsa
Combine 2 seeded chopped tomatoes, 1 finely
chopped red onion, ¼ cup chopped fresh coriander
and 1 tablespoon each of lime juice and olive oil.
serves 4
per serving 4.6g fat; 231kJ (55 cal)

coriander chilli sauce
Blend or process 6 chopped green onions, 2 garlic
cloves, 2 red thai chillies, 1 tablespoon chopped
fresh coriander root and 1½ tablespoons brown
sugar until chopped finely. Add 1½ tablespoons
fish sauce and 2 tablespoons lime juice.
serves 4
per serving 0.1g fat; 125kJ (30 cal)

lemon grass pesto
Blend or process ¼ cup roasted unsalted peanuts,
2 red thai chillies, 1 chopped lemon grass stalk,
½ cup fresh coriander leaves, ⅓ cup peanut oil and
1 tablespoon lemon juice until mixture forms a paste.
serves 4
per serving 22.7g fat; 905kJ (216 cal)

thai-style salmon salad with lime dressing

415g can red salmon, drained
1 lebanese cucumber (130g), sliced
4 large french shallots (100g), sliced
200g cherry tomatoes, halved
2 baby cos lettuce
8 mint leaves
8 basil leaves, torn
lime dressing
$1/4$ cup (60ml) lime juice
1 tablespoon soy sauce
1 teaspoon fish sauce
1 teaspoon brown sugar
$1/4$ teaspoon sesame oil
1 fresh red thai chilli, seeded, chopped

Break salmon into chunks. Toss the remaining ingredients in a large bowl. Add salmon and drizzle with lime dressing.
Lime dressing Combine ingredients in a screw-topped jar; shake well.

serves 4
per serving 11.2g fat; 937kJ (224 cal)
on the table in 20 minutes

spaghetti with puttanesca sauce

2 tablespoons olive oil
2 cloves garlic, crushed
4 medium tomatoes (760g), chopped coarsely
$1/2$ cup chopped fresh flat-leaf parsley
12 stuffed green olives, sliced thinly
45g can anchovy fillets, drained, chopped finely
1 tablespoon finely shredded fresh basil
pinch chilli powder
375g spaghetti

Heat oil in medium frying pan; cook garlic
until it just changes colour. Add tomato,
parsley, olives, anchovy, basil and chilli
powder; cook, stirring, 5 minutes.
Meanwhile, cook pasta in large saucepan
of boiling water until tender; drain. Combine
sauce and pasta.

serves 4
per serving 12g fat; 1854kJ (443 cal)
on the table in 30 minutes

tuna dip

180g can sandwich tuna in oil
1/2 small white onion (40g), chopped finely
30g soft butter
1 teaspoon grated lemon rind
2 teaspoons lemon juice
1 clove garlic, crushed
2 teaspoons drained capers, chopped
1 tablespoon chopped fresh basil
2 teaspoons chopped fresh oregano

Blend or process undrained tuna, onion, butter, rind, juice and garlic until smooth; transfer mixture to medium bowl. Add capers and herbs; mix well.
Serve with fresh crusty bread, if desired.

makes 1 1/4 cups (265g)
per tablespoon 2.8g fat; 147kJ (35 cal)
on the table in 10 minutes

salmon patties with cucumber and rocket salad

4 medium potatoes (800g), chopped coarsely
415g can red salmon, drained, flaked
4 green onions, chopped coarsely
$1/4$ teaspoon finely grated lime rind
$1/2$ cup (75g) plain flour
2 eggs, beaten lightly
1 cup (100g) packaged breadcrumbs
vegetable oil, for shallow-frying
3 lebanese cucumbers (390g)
100g baby rocket leaves
2 fresh red thai chillies, seeded, chopped finely
2 tablespoons lime juice

Boil, steam or microwave potato until tender;
drain. Mash potato in medium bowl until smooth;
cool 5 minutes. Add salmon, onion and rind;
stir until well combined.
Using hands, shape salmon mixture into
eight patties. Coat each patty with flour,
shaking off excess; dip patties in egg then
coat evenly with breadcrumbs.
Heat oil in large frying pan; cook patties,
in batches, until browned both sides.
Using a vegetable peeler, slice cucumbers,
lengthways, as thinly as possible. Place
cucumber ribbons in large bowl with rocket,
chilli and juice; toss gently to combine.
Serve with salmon patties.

serves 4
per serving 32.8g fat; 2803kJ (670 cal)
on the table in 45 minutes

pissaladière

Pissaladière, a specialty of southern France, is a flaky, pizza-like tart topped with anchovies, onion and olives.

1 tablespoon olive oil
20g butter
2 cloves garlic, crushed
4 large brown onions (800g), sliced thinly
1 sprig fresh thyme
1 tablespoon drained baby capers
20 canned anchovy fillets (75g), chopped coarsely
1½ sheets ready rolled frozen shortcrust pastry, thawed
1 cup (250ml) bottled tomato pasta sauce
1 tablespoon chopped fresh flat-leaf parsley
½ cup (60g) seeded black olives

Preheat oven to moderately hot. Lightly grease 22cm-round loose-based flan tin. Heat oil and butter in large frying pan; cook garlic, onion and thyme, covered, over low heat, stirring occasionally, 30 minutes or until onion is soft but not browned. Remove thyme; stir in capers and half the anchovy.

Meanwhile, brush a little water along one edge of pastry, join pastry sheets together along watered edge, pressing gently to seal. Lift pastry into prepared tin, ease into sides; trim edges. Lightly prick base with fork, cover pastry with baking paper and fill with rice or dried beans; place on oven tray. Bake pastry in moderately hot oven 20 minutes. Remove paper and rice carefully from pastry case; bake 5 minutes or until lightly browned.

Spread pastry case with combined tomato sauce and parsley. Spread onion mixture over tomato mixture; sprinkle top with remaining anchovy and olives. Bake in moderately hot oven about 10 minutes or until heated through.

serves 4
per serving 28.4g fat; 2117kJ (506 cal)
on the table in 50 minutes

niçoise salad

Canned cooked white beans can have one of several different names on the label, such as cannellini, butter or haricot. There is little difference in taste or texture among any of these small, slightly kidney-shaped white beans, and any would be suitable for this salad.

3 x 125g cans tuna slices in springwater, drained
1 medium red onion (170g), sliced thinly
250g baby spinach leaves, trimmed
300g can white beans, rinsed, drained
150g yellow teardrop tomatoes, halved
$1/2$ cup (80g) kalamata olives, seeded
4 hard-boiled eggs, shelled, quartered
dressing
$1/2$ cup (125ml) olive oil
$1/4$ cup (60ml) lemon juice
1 clove garlic, crushed
1 teaspoon coarsely chopped fresh lemon thyme
2 teaspoons dijon mustard
$1/4$ teaspoon sugar

Combine ingredients in large bowl.
Pour dressing over salad mixture; toss gently to combine.
Dressing Combine ingredients in a screw-topped jar; shake well.

serves 4
per serving 36.5g fat; 2011kJ (480 cal)
on the table in 15 minutes

smoked trout pâté

400g whole smoked trout
1 egg yolk
2 teaspoons white vinegar
2 teaspoons mustard powder
1 tablespoon lemon juice
$1/4$ teaspoon lemon pepper seasoning
$1/3$ cup (80ml) extra light olive oil

Remove skin and bones from trout;
coarsely flake flesh.
Blend or process egg yolk, vinegar, mustard,
juice and lemon pepper until smooth. With
motor operating, add oil gradually in a thin
stream. Add trout; blend until smooth.

serves 4
per serving 21.6g fat; 984kJ (235 cal)
on the table in 20 minutes

salmon and herb soufflés

210g can red salmon, drained, flaked
1 tablespoon chopped fresh chives
1 tablespoon chopped fresh flat-leaf parsley
pinch cayenne pepper
20g butter
1 tablespoon plain flour
$^1/_2$ cup (125ml) milk
2 egg whites

Preheat oven to moderate. Grease two
soufflé (1 cup/250ml) dishes.
Combine salmon, herbs and pepper in
medium bowl; mix well.
Heat butter in small saucepan, stir in flour;
cook until bubbling, remove from heat. Gradually
stir in milk; stir over heat until sauce boils and
thickens. Stir sauce into salmon mixture.
Beat egg whites until soft peaks form; fold into
salmon mixture. Spoon mixture into prepared
dishes. Bake in moderate oven about 20 minutes
or until risen and well browned; serve immediately.

serves 2
per serving 20.9g fat; 1321kJ (315 cal)
on the table in 35 minutes

kedgeree

You will need approximately 1¼ cups (250g) of uncooked long-grain rice for this recipe.

1 tablespoon vegetable oil
1 medium brown onion (150g), chopped finely
1 tablespoon mild curry paste
3 cups cooked long-grain white rice
415g can pink salmon, drained, flaked
¼ cup (60ml) cream
1 hard-boiled egg
2 tablespoons chopped fresh flat-leaf parsley

Heat oil in large saucepan; cook onion, stirring, until soft. Add curry paste; cook, stirring, until fragrant. Stir in rice, salmon and cream; cook, stirring, until hot.
Cut egg into 8 wedges and gently stir through kedgeree; sprinkle with parsley to serve.

serves 4
per serving 20g fat; 1891kJ (452 cal)
on the table in 20 minutes

anchovy pizza

2 teaspoons olive oil
1 medium brown onion (150g), chopped finely
1 clove garlic, crushed
410g can whole tomatoes
1 tablespoon tomato paste
1 tablespoon chopped fresh oregano
1 teaspoon sugar
25cm-round pizza base
1¼ cups (125g) grated mozzarella cheese
2 tablespoons grated parmesan cheese
45g can anchovy fillets, drained
1 small red capsicum (150g), sliced thinly
3 button mushrooms, sliced thinly
½ cup (60g) seeded black olives, halved
¼ cup small fresh basil leaves

Preheat oven to hot. Heat oil in large frying
pan; cook onion and garlic until onion is soft.
Add undrained, crushed tomatoes, paste,
oregano and sugar. Bring to a boil; reduce heat.
Simmer, uncovered, stirring occasionally,
about 10 minutes or until sauce is thick.
Spread sauce over pizza base. Combine
cheeses in small bowl; sprinkle half of the
cheese mixture over pizza. Top with anchovy,
capsicum and mushrooms. Sprinkle with olives
and remaining cheese. Bake in hot oven about
15 minutes or until base is golden brown.
Sprinkle with basil to serve.

serves 4
per serving 13.6g fat; 1548kJ (370 cal)
on the table in 40 minutes

calamari and vegetable salad

45g can anchovy fillets, drained
2 cloves garlic, crushed
1 tablespoon chopped fresh flat-leaf parsley
1/4 cup (60ml) olive oil
400g frozen crumbed calamari rings
vegetable oil, for deep-frying
3 medium tomatoes (570g), quartered
1 tablespoon chopped fresh basil
1 medium green capsicum (200g), sliced thinly
1 medium avocado (250g), chopped coarsely
1 small green cucumber (130g), sliced thinly
1/2 cup (60g) seeded black olives
1 tablespoon white vinegar
4 large lettuce leaves, torn

Place anchovy in small bowl; add half of the
garlic, parsley and 1 tablespoon of the olive oil.
Let stand while preparing the salad.
Deep-fry calamari, in batches, in hot vegetable
oil until golden brown; drain on absorbent paper.
Combine tomato, remaining garlic, basil,
capsicum, avocado, cucumber and olives in
large bowl. Combine remaining oil and vinegar in
medium jug. Pour over salad; toss to combine.
Place lettuce in serving bowl; top with salad,
calamari and anchovy mixture.

serves 4
per serving 47.8g fat; 2514kJ (601 cal)
on the table in 35 minutes

seafood rice

You will need about 1 1/3 cups (265g) of uncooked rice for this recipe.

30g butter
500g seafood marinara mix
1 tablespoon olive oil
1 clove garlic, crushed
200g button mushrooms, sliced thinly
100g snow peas, sliced thinly
4 green onions, chopped finely
4 slices smoked salmon (75g), chopped coarsely
4 cups cooked rice
2 tablespoons chopped fresh flat-leaf parsley
1/4 cup (60ml) lemon juice
1/4 cup (20g) grated parmesan cheese

Heat butter in large frying pan. Cook marinara mix, stirring, until tender; remove marinara mix from pan.
Heat oil in same pan; cook garlic, mushrooms and snow peas, stirring, until snow peas are tender. Add marinara mix, onion, salmon, rice, parsley and juice; stir until heated through. Serve sprinkled with cheese.

serves 4
per serving 17.5g fat; 2379kJ (568 cal)
on the table in 30 minutes

pea flapjacks with smoked trout

400g whole smoked trout
1/2 cup (75g) plain flour
1/2 cup (75g) self-raising flour
1/4 teaspoon bicarbonate
　of soda
2/3 cup (160ml) buttermilk
1/3 cup (80ml) milk
1/2 cup (60g) frozen peas,
　thawed, drained
1 tablespoon chopped
　fresh flat-leaf parsley
2 tablespoons chopped
　fresh chives
1 egg white
1/4 cup (60g) sour cream
pickled cucumber
2 lebanese
　cucumbers (260g)
1 small red capsicum
　(150g), chopped finely
1/4 cup (60ml) water
1/4 cup (55g) sugar
1/2 cup (125ml) white vinegar

Remove skin and bones from trout; coarsely flake flesh.

Sift flours and soda into large bowl; gradually whisk in combined buttermilk, milk, peas, parsley and half of the chives.

Beat egg white in small bowl with rotary or electric mixer until soft peaks form; fold egg white into batter. Pour 1/3-cup portions (80ml) of the batter into large heated oiled non-stick frying pan; cook flapjacks, in batches, until browned lightly on both sides.

Combine sour cream and remaining chives in small bowl. Serve warm flapjacks topped with trout, pickled cucumber and sour cream mixture.

Pickled cucumber Using vegetable peeler, slice cucumber lengthways into ribbons. Combine cucumber in medium bowl with capsicum. Combine the water and sugar in small saucepan; stir over low heat until sugar dissolves. Bring to a boil; reduce heat. Simmer, uncovered, about 5 minutes or until thickened slightly. Add vinegar to sugar syrup; pour hot syrup over cucumber mixture.

serves 6
per serving 6.4g fat; 1011kJ (241 cal)
on the table in 45 minutes

fettuccine with creamy salmon and dill sauce

375g fettuccine
1/2 cup (120g) light sour cream
2 tablespoons lemon juice
415g can red salmon, drained
1 small red onion (100g), sliced thinly
1/4 cup loosely packed fresh dill
2 tablespoons drained small capers
1 tablespoon grated lemon rind

Cook pasta in large saucepan of boiling water, uncovered, until tender; drain.
Meanwhile, combine sour cream and juice in small bowl. Break the salmon into chunks. Toss hot pasta with sour cream mixture, salmon, onion, dill and capers until combined.
Serve topped with lemon rind.

serves 4
per serving 17.1g fat; 2314kJ (553 cal)
on the table in 20 minutes

prawn pick-me-ups

*Easy does it with these delicious accompaniments to prawns.
Each recipe, served with 1kg of cooked prawns, is enough to
feed four lucky people – just peel, then dip or drizzle and eat!*

lemon garlic dressing

Combine ½ cup olive oil, ¼ cup lemon juice,
1 crushed garlic clove and 1 teaspoon sugar.
serves 4
per serving 28.5g fat; 1093kJ (261 calories)

lime and dill mayonnaise

Combine ½ cup mayonnaise and 1 tablespoon each
of lime juice and chopped fresh dill; season to taste.
serves 4
per serving 12.9g fat; 576kJ (138 cal)

lime and coriander dressing

Blend or process 1 garlic clove, ⅓ cup lime juice,
2 tablespoons each of fish sauce, chopped fresh
coriander and chopped fresh mint, and ¼ cup
peanut oil until well combined.
serves 4
per serving 13.8g fat; 552kJ (132 cal)

cocktail sauce

Combine 1 cup mayonnaise, ⅓ cup tomato sauce,
and ½ teaspoon each of worcestershire sauce and
chilli sauce.
serves 4
per serving 24g fat; 1240kJ (296 cal)

avocado sauce
Blend or process 1 avocado, 1 tablespoon
peanut oil, 2 tablespoons each of lime juice and
cream, and ½ teaspoon sugar until smooth.
serves 4
per serving 16.9g fat; 663kJ (158 cal)

horseradish cream
Combine 1 cup sour cream and 2 tablespoons
prepared horseradish cream.
serves 4
per serving 25g fat; 1007kJ (240 cal)

thai dressing
Combine ⅓ cup sweet chilli sauce, ½ cup lime juice,
1 tablespoon fish sauce, 2 teaspoons each of finely
chopped fresh lemon grass and grated fresh ginger,
2 tablespoons chopped fresh coriander and
½ cup chopped fresh mint.
serves 4
per serving 0.7g fat; 149kJ (36 cal)

tomato vinaigrette
Blend or process 3 peeled seeded tomatoes,
2 chopped green onions, ⅓ cup each of red wine
vinegar and sweet chilli sauce, 2 garlic cloves,
1 teaspoon each of seeded mustard, sugar and
cracked pepper, and ¼ cup chopped fresh parsley
until almost smooth.
serves 4
per serving 0.7g fat; 161kJ (39 cal)

american crab cakes

2 x 170g cans crab meat, drained
1 egg, beaten lightly
6 green onions, sliced thinly
2 tablespoons mayonnaise
1 tablespoon dijon mustard
1 cup (70g) fresh breadcrumbs
1 tablespoon worcestershire sauce
1 tablespoon chopped fresh flat-leaf parsley
$1/4$ teaspoon sweet paprika
$1/4$ cup (25g) packaged breadcrumbs
$1/4$ cup (60ml) vegetable oil

Combine crab, egg, onion, mayonnaise, mustard, fresh breadcrumbs, sauce, parsley and paprika in medium bowl. Shape mixture into four patties; coat in packaged breadcrumbs. **Heat** oil in medium frying pan; cook patties until browned both sides and cooked through.

makes 4
per crab cake 19.5g fat; 1289kJ (308 cal)
on the table in 30 minutes
tip The crab cakes will hold together a little better if you have time to refrigerate the patties for 1 hour prior to cooking.

chilli tuna pasta salad

300g large pasta shells
250g green beans, halved
2 x 185g cans tuna in chilli oil
1/3 cup chopped fresh flat-leaf parsley
1/3 cup torn fresh basil leaves
2 tablespoons drained baby capers
150g baby rocket leaves
dressing
1/4 cup (60ml) olive oil
1/4 cup (60ml) lemon juice
2 cloves garlic, crushed
2 teaspoons sugar

Cook pasta in large saucepan of boiling water,
uncovered, until just tender; drain. Rinse pasta
under cold water; drain.

Meanwhile, boil, steam or microwave beans
until just tender; drain. Drain tuna over small bowl,
reserve the chilli oil for dressing. Flake tuna into
large chunks with a fork.

Combine pasta, beans, tuna, herbs and capers
in large bowl, drizzle with dressing. Serve salad
topped with rocket leaves.

Dressing Combine ingredients with reserved
chilli oil in a screw-topped jar; shake well.

serves 6
per serving 24.3g fat; 1890kJ (451 cal)
on the table in 30 minutes

bagna cauda

2²/₃ cups (600ml)
  thickened cream
60g butter
45g can anchovy fillets,
  drained, chopped
  very finely
2 cloves garlic, crushed

Place cream in small saucepan; bring to a boil. Reduce heat to low; simmer, uncovered, stirring frequently, about 15 minutes or until cream has thickened.

Melt butter over low heat in medium saucepan (do not brown butter), add anchovy and garlic; cook, stirring, until mixture is combined and forms a paste.

Stir hot cream into anchovy mixture until well combined; serve warm.

makes 2³/₄ cups (825g)
per tablespoon 8.5g fat; 336kJ (80 cal)
on the table in 35 minutes

traditional tapenade

1 tablespoon
  drained capers
3 canned anchovy
  fillets, drained
½ cup (60g) seeded
  black olives
¼ cup (60ml) olive oil

Blend or process combined ingredients until well combined.

makes ½ cup (125g)
per tablespoon 9.4g fat; 399kJ (95 cal)
on the table in 5 minutes

smoked salmon on chilli corn fritters

Frozen corn can be substituted for fresh, if preferred.

1¼ cups (300g) sour cream
1 small red onion (100g), chopped finely
¼ cup chopped fresh chives
¼ cup chopped fresh dill
1 cob of corn (400g)
1 egg, beaten lightly
⅓ cup (50g) self-raising flour
1½ tablespoons milk
1 fresh red thai chilli, seeded, chopped finely
1 tablespoon chopped fresh coriander
vegetable oil, for shallow-frying
200g smoked salmon slices

Combine sour cream, onion, chives and dill in small bowl.

Remove and discard husk and silk from corn; cut kernels from cob. Boil, steam or microwave kernels until just tender, drain on absorbent paper.

Combine egg and flour in small bowl; gradually stir in milk. Add corn, chilli and coriander; stir to combine.

Heat oil in medium frying pan; cook heaped tablespoons of corn mixture, one at a time, until browned both sides and cooked through. Drain on absorbent paper (you will need eight fritters).

Place two fritters on each serving plate; top each serving with equal amounts of sour cream mixture, then salmon slices.

serves 4
per serving 40.5g fat; 2265kJ (541 cal)
on the table in 40 minutes

pasta with tuna and pimientos

300g pasta shells
2 tablespoons olive oil
1 medium brown onion (150g), chopped finely
4 cloves garlic, crushed
410g can red pimientos, drained, sliced thinly
425g can tuna, drained, flaked
1 cup (250ml) water
1/4 cup (60ml) lemon juice
1/4 cup loosely packed fresh basil leaves, torn

Cook pasta in large saucepan of boiling water, uncovered, until just tender; drain.
Meanwhile, heat oil in large frying pan; cook onion and garlic, stirring, until onion is soft.
Stir in pimiento, tuna, the water and juice; bring to a boil. Remove from heat; stir in basil. Top pasta with sauce.

serves 4
per serving 10.9g fat; 1910kJ (457 cal)
on the table in 20 minutes

tunisian tuna salad

2 hard-boiled eggs, shelled, chopped finely
1 medium green capsicum (200g),
    chopped finely
2 medium tomatoes (380g), seeded, chopped finely
4 green onions, chopped finely
2 large canned anchovy fillets, drained,
    chopped finely
10 seeded green olives (30g), chopped finely
2 fresh red thai chillies, seeded, chopped finely
1 tablespoon finely chopped fresh mint
180g can tuna chunks in springwater,
    drained, flaked
1 tablespoon drained baby capers
caraway-seed dressing
2 tablespoons olive oil
1 clove garlic, crushed
1 teaspoon coriander seeds
1 teaspoon caraway seeds
1 tablespoon lemon juice
2 tablespoons red wine vinegar

Combine ingredients in medium bowl;
drizzle caraway-seed dressing over salad,
toss gently to combine.
Caraway-seed dressing Heat oil in small
frying pan, add garlic and seeds; cook, stirring,
until fragrant. Stir in juice and vinegar.

serves 4
per serving 13.3g fat; 825kJ (197 cal)
on the table in 30 minutes

ricotta tuna loaf with salsa verde

1 cup (200g) ricotta cheese
3 eggs
4 green onions, chopped finely
1 cup (70g) stale breadcrumbs
425g can tuna in oil, drained, flaked
salsa verde
1 cup firmly packed fresh flat-leaf parsley
1 clove garlic, crushed
1 tablespoon drained capers
2 tablespoons coarsely chopped, drained gherkins
8 canned anchovy fillets, drained
1 teaspoon grated lemon rind
1/3 cup (80ml) olive oil

Preheat oven to moderate. Grease
14cm x 21cm loaf pan. Line base and
two opposite sides with baking paper.
Combine ricotta and eggs in medium bowl,
whisk until smooth. Stir in onion, breadcrumbs
and tuna. Pour mixture into prepared pan.
Bake, uncovered, in moderate oven about
40 minutes or until firm. Stand 5 minutes before
turning out. Serve sliced with salsa verde.
Salsa verde Blend or process parsley, garlic,
capers, gherkin, anchovy and rind until well
combined. Gradually pour in oil while motor
is operating. Process until almost smooth.

serves 4
per serving 41g fat; 2388kJ (570 cal)
on the table in 50 minutes

smoked cod with rocket pesto on fettuccine

375g fettuccine
500g smoked cod fillets
rocket pesto
150g baby rocket leaves
2 cloves garlic, crushed
$1/4$ cup (40g) toasted pine nuts
$1/4$ cup (35g) toasted pistachios
2 tablespoons lemon juice
$1/2$ cup (40g) coarsely grated parmesan cheese
$3/4$ cup (180ml) olive oil

Cook pasta in large saucepan of boiling
water, uncovered, until tender; drain.
Meanwhile, cook fish in large non-stick
frying pan until browned both sides; cool
5 minutes then flake with fork into large bowl.
Place pasta in large bowl with fish and
rocket pesto; toss gently to combine.
Rocket pesto Blend or process
ingredients to form a paste.

serves 4
per serving 58.2g fat; 4007kJ (957 cal)
on the table in 30 minutes

taramasalata

Tarama is salted, dried roe of the grey mullet fish,
available from continental delicatessens
and some supermarkets.

1 large old potato (300g), peeled, chopped
100g tarama
1 tablespoon lemon juice
$1/4$ cup (60ml) white vinegar
$1/2$ small white onion (40g), grated finely
$3/4$ cup (180ml) olive oil

Boil, steam or microwave potato until
tender; drain. Mash potato, tarama, juice,
vinegar, onion and oil until smooth.

makes 2$1/2$ cups (600g)
per tablespoon 6g fat; 260kJ (62 cal)
on the table in 20 minutes

smoked salmon and caviar salad

Kipflers are small, bumpy, finger-shaped potatoes with a nutty flavour.

1.2kg kipfler potatoes
1 tablespoon olive oil
500g fresh asparagus, trimmed
400g finely sliced smoked salmon
100g mesclun
25g red caviar
avocado puree
1 small avocado (200g)
$1/4$ cup (60g) sour cream
1 tablespoon chopped fresh dill
2 tablespoons lime juice

Preheat oven to very hot. Boil, steam or microwave potatoes until just tender; drain.
Halve potatoes; place, cut-side up, on lightly oiled oven tray, drizzle with oil. Bake, uncovered, in very hot oven about 15 minutes or until crisp and brown, turning occasionally.
Meanwhile, boil, steam or microwave asparagus until just tender; drain, cut spears in half crossways.
Cut salmon slices into thin strips. Divide avocado puree among serving plates; top with potato, mesclun, asparagus, salmon and caviar.
Avocado puree Halve avocado; discard stone, chop flesh coarsely. Blend or process avocado with remaining ingredients until smooth.

serves 4
per serving 24g fat; 2213kJ (529 cal)
on the table in 45 minutes

tuna and white bean salad

Canned cooked white beans can have one of several different names on the label, such as cannellini, butter or haricot. There is little difference in taste or texture among any of these small, slightly kidney-shaped white beans, and any would be suitable for this salad.

2 x 300g cans white beans, rinsed, drained
425g can tuna chunks in springwater, drained, flaked
1 medium red onion (170g), sliced thinly
1/2 cup chopped fresh flat-leaf parsley
1 tablespoon chopped fresh oregano
250g cherry tomatoes, quartered
2 tablespoons olive oil
1 tablespoon white vinegar
2 teaspoons finely grated lemon rind
2 tablespoons lemon juice
2 cloves garlic, crushed
1 long loaf pide

Combine beans and tuna in large bowl with onion, parsley, oregano and tomato; toss gently with combined oil, vinegar, rind, juice and garlic.
Quarter bread crossways; slice pieces in half horizontally. Cut bread again, on the diagonal, to make 16 triangles; toast triangles, cut-side up.
Place one triangle, toasted-side up, on each serving plate; top with salad, then remaining triangles.

serves 8
per serving 7.5g fat; 1116kJ (267 cal)
on the table in 20 minutes

smoked salmon rice paper rolls

1 medium carrot (120g)
1 lebanese cucumber (130g), halved, seeded
16 x 16cm-round rice paper sheets
16 slices (300g) smoked salmon
1 large avocado (320g), sliced
4 green onions, sliced
dipping sauce
1/2 cup (125ml) sweet chilli sauce
1/4 cup (60ml) lime juice
2 tablespoons chopped fresh coriander
2 tablespoons chopped fresh mint

Cut carrot and cucumber into long thin strips.
Place 1 sheet of rice paper in bowl of warm
water until just softened; lift from water carefully,
place on board. Place a slice of salmon, a slice
of avocado and a little of the carrot, cucumber
and onion on one end of sheet. Roll once,
fold in sides, roll up to enclose filling.
Repeat with remaining rice paper, salmon,
avocado, carrot, cucumber and onion.
Serve rolls with dipping sauce.
Dipping sauce Combine ingredients in small bowl.

makes 16
per roll 4.3g fat; 372kJ (89 cal)
on the table in 40 minutes

crab rolls with chilli plum sauce

2 teaspoons peanut oil
1 teaspoon grated
   fresh ginger
2 cloves garlic, crushed
4 green onions, chopped
1/2 small red capsicum (75g),
   chopped finely
2 x 170g cans crab
   meat, drained
1/4 cup (50g) drained water
   chestnuts, chopped finely
1 teaspoon sugar
25 small spring roll
   wrappers
vegetable oil,
   for deep-frying
chilli plum sauce
2 teaspoons peanut oil
1 clove garlic, crushed
1 teaspoon grated
   fresh ginger
1/3 cup (80ml) chinese
   plum sauce
1/3 cup (80ml) mild sweet
   chilli sauce
1 tablespoon brown sugar
2/3 cup (160ml)
   chicken stock

Heat oil in medium frying pan, add ginger, garlic, onion and capsicum; cook, stirring, until capsicum is soft, cool 5 minutes. Stir in crab, chestnuts and sugar.

Place 1 tablespoon crab mixture across a corner of 1 spring roll wrapper; brush edges with a little water, fold in sides, roll up to enclose filling. Repeat with remaining crab mixture and wrappers.

Deep-fry crab rolls in hot oil, in batches, until browned; drain on absorbent paper. Serve with chilli plum sauce.

Chilli plum sauce Heat oil in small saucepan, add garlic and ginger; cook, stirring, until fragrant. Add remaining ingredients; simmer, uncovered, about 10 minutes or until reduced to 1 cup (250ml).

makes 25 rolls
per roll 2.5g fat; 241kJ (57 cal)
on the table in 40 minutes

glossary

bicarbonate of soda also known as baking soda.

breadcrumbs
packaged: purchased, fine, crunchy white breadcrumbs.
stale: one- or two-day-old bread made into crumbs by grating, blending or processing.

butter use salted or unsalted (sweet) butter; 125g is equal to one stick of butter.

buttermilk sold alongside fresh milk products in supermarkets; despite its name, is low in fat. Commercially made similarly to yogurt.

button mushrooms small, cultivated white mushrooms with a mild flavour.

calamari rings a type of squid, cleaned and cut into rings.

capers the grey-green buds of a warm-climate shrub; sold either dried and salted or pickled in a vinegar brine.

capsicum also known as bell pepper or, simply, pepper. Discard seeds and membranes before use.

caraway seeds the seeds of a member of the parsley family; used in sweet and savoury dishes.

cayenne pepper an extremely hot red chilli, purchased dried and ground.

cheese
mozzarella: soft, spun-curd cheese traditionally made from water buffalo milk. Cow-milk versions of this product, commonly known as pizza cheese, are now available.
parmesan: also known as parmigiano, parmesan is a hard, grainy cow-milk cheese, aged for up to two years.

ricotta: a sweet, moist, cow-milk cheese, made from whey, with a fat content of around 8.5% and a slightly grainy texture.

chilli
powder: the Asian variety is the hottest, made from ground chillies; use as a substitute for fresh chillies in the proportion of ½ teaspoon chilli powder to 1 medium chopped fresh chilli.
sweet chilli sauce: a mild, Thai-style sauce made from red chillies, sugar, garlic and vinegar.
thai: small, hot chillies; bright-red to dark-green in colour.

cos lettuce also known as roma lettuce; has crisp elongated leaves. Baby cos lettuce is also available.

crème fraîche fermented cream that has a slightly nutty, tangy flavour and velvety rich texture.

curry paste commercially prepared paste available in various strengths and flavours; use whichever paste best suits your spice tolerance.

egg some recipes use raw or barely-cooked eggs; show caution if salmonella is a problem in your area.

fish sauce also called nam pla or nuoc nam; made from pulverised, salted, fermented fish, most often anchovies. Has a strong taste; use sparingly.

flour
plain: also known as all-purpose flour; made from wheat.
self raising: plain flour sifted with baking powder in the proportion of 1 cup flour to 2 teaspoons baking powder.

french shallot a member of the onion family; grows in a cluster of bulbs, much like garlic.

ginger also known as green or root ginger; the thick gnarled root of a tropical plant. Can be kept, peeled and covered with dry sherry, in a jar in the refrigerator, or frozen in an airtight container.

green beans sometimes called french or string beans (although the tough string they once had has generally been bred out of them), this long fresh bean is consumed pod and all.

horseradish cream a creamy prepared paste of grated horseradish, vinegar, oil and sugar.

kalamata olive a dark olive preserved in brine.

lebanese cucumber long, slender and thin-skinned; this variety is also known as the European or burpless cucumber.

lemon pepper seasoning a mix of crushed black pepper, lemon, herbs and spices.

mayonnaise we used bottled whole-egg mayonnaise unless otherwise specified.

mesclun also known as salad mix or gourmet salad mix; a mixture of assorted young lettuce and other green leaves.

mustard
dijon: a pale-brown, distinctively flavoured, fairly mild French mustard.
powder: finely ground white (yellow) mustard seeds.

wholegrain: also known as seeded. A coarse-grain mustard made from crushed mustard seeds and dijon-style French mustard.

oil

olive: made from ripened olives. Extra virgin and virgin are the best, while extra light or light refers to taste not fat levels.

peanut: pressed from ground peanuts; most commonly used oil in Asian cooking because of its high smoke point.

sesame: made from roasted, crushed white sesame seeds; used for its flavour, not as a cooking medium.

vegetable: any of a number of oils sourced from plants rather than animal fats.

onion

green: also known as scallion or (incorrectly) shallot; an immature onion picked before the bulb has formed, having a long, bright-green edible stalk.

red: also known as spanish, red spanish or bermuda onion; a sweet-flavoured, large, purple-red onion.

paprika ground dried red capsicum (bell pepper), available sweet or hot.

pide turkish bread that comes in long flat loaves as well as individual rounds; made from wheat flour and sprinkled with sesame or black onion seeds.

pimientos canned or bottled capsicums.

pine nuts also known as pignoli; small, cream-coloured kernels obtained from the cones of some pine trees.

pistachio pale-green, delicately flavoured nut inside hard off-white shell.

ready-rolled frozen shortcrust pastry
packaged sheets of frozen shortcrust pastry; available from supermarkets.

rice paper sheets made from ground rice flour, salt and water; sold packaged in either round or square pieces.

rice wine a sweet, low-alcohol wine, gold in colour, that is made from fermented rice.

rocket also known as arugula, rugula and rucola; a peppery-tasting green leaf. Baby rocket leaves are also available.

seafood marinara mix a mixture of uncooked, chopped seafood available from fish retailers.

snow peas also called mange tout ("eat all"). Snow pea tendrils, the shoots of the plant, are sold by green grocers.

soy sauce made from fermented soy beans.

spinach also known as English spinach and, incorrectly, silverbeet.

spring roll wrappers also known as egg roll wrappers; available in various sizes. Purchase fresh or frozen from Asian food stores. Use for making gow gee and samosas as well as spring rolls.

stock stock cubes, powder or concentrated liquid can be used. As a guide, 1 teaspoon of stock powder or 1 small crumbled stock cube or 1 portion stock concentrate mixed with 1 cup (250ml) water will give a fairly strong stock. Be aware of the salt and fat content of stocks.

sugar, brown a soft, finely granulated sugar that retains molasses for its characteristic colour and flavour.

tarama salted, dried roe of the grey mullet fish.

tomato

paste: triple-concentrated tomato puree used to flavour soups, stews and sauces.

cherry: also known as Tiny Tim or Tom Thumb tomatoes; small and round.

yellow teardrop: small, yellow, pear-shaped tomatoes.

water chestnuts resemble chestnuts in appearance, hence the English name. They are small brown tubers with a crisp, white, nutty-tasting flesh.

worcestershire sauce a thin, dark-brown, spicy sauce used as a seasoning for meat, gravies and cocktails, as well as a condiment.

index

american crab cakes 34
anchovy butter 2
anchovy pizza 23
avocado sauce 33
bagna cauda 38
calamari and vegetable salad 24
chilli corn fritters,
    smoked salmon on 41
chilli lime dressing 2
chilli plum sauce,
    crab rolls with 58
chilli tuna pasta salad 37
cocktail sauce 32
coriander chilli sauce 3
crab cakes, american 34
crab rolls with
    chilli plum sauce 58
creamy salmon and dill sauce,
    fettuccine with 31
cucumber and rocket salad,
    salmon patties with 11
dill and caper dressing 2
dip, tuna 8
dressing, chilli lime 2
dressing, dill and caper 2
dressing, lemon garlic 32
dressing, lime and coriander 32
dressing, thai 33
fettuccine, smoked cod
    with rocket pesto on 49
fettuccine with creamy
    salmon and dill sauce 31
flapjacks, pea, with
    smoked trout 28
gremolata, walnut 3
horseradish cream 33
kedgeree 20
lemon garlic dressing 32
lemon grass pesto 3
lime and coriander dressing 32
lime and dill mayonnaise 32
mayonnaise, lime and dill 32
niçoise salad 15
olive paste 2
pasta salad, chilli tuna 37
pasta with tuna and pimientos 42

pâté, smoked trout 16
pea flapjacks with
    smoked trout 28
pesto, lemon grass 3
pesto, rocket, smoked cod with,
    on fettuccine 49
pissaladière 12
pizza, anchovy 23
puttanesca sauce,
    spaghetti with 7
rice paper rolls,
    smoked salmon 57
rice, seafood 27
ricotta tuna loaf with
    salsa verde 46
rocket pesto, smoked cod
    with, on fettuccine 49
salad, calamari and
    vegetable 24
salad, chilli tuna pasta 37
salad, cucumber and rocket,
    salmon patties with 11
salad, niçoise 15
salad, smoked salmon
    and caviar 53
salad, thai-style salmon,
    with lime dressing 4
salad, tuna and white bean 54
salad, tunisian tuna 45
salmon and dill sauce, creamy,
    fettuccine with 31
salmon and herb soufflés 19
salmon patties with cucumber
    and rocket salad 11
salmon salad, thai-style,
    with lime dressing 4
salsa, tomato and coriander 3
salsa verde, ricotta tuna
    loaf with 46
seafood rice 27
smoked cod with rocket pesto
    on fettuccine 49
smoked salmon and
    caviar salad 53
smoked salmon on
    chilli corn fritters 41

smoked salmon
    rice paper rolls 57
smoked trout pâté 16
smoked trout, pea
    flapjacks with 28
soufflés, salmon and herb 19
spaghetti with
    puttanesca sauce 7
tapenade, traditional 39
taramasalata 50
thai dressing 33
thai-style salmon salad
    with lime dressing 4
tomato and coriander salsa 3
tomato vinaigrette 33
traditional tapenade 39
tuna and pimientos,
    pasta with 42
tuna and white bean salad 54
tuna dip 8
tuna pasta salad, chilli 37
tunisian tuna salad 45
vinaigrette, tomato 33
walnut gremolata 3

facts & figures

These conversions are approximate only, but the difference between an exact and the approximate conversion of various liquid and dry measures is minimal and will not affect your cooking results.

Note: NZ, Canada, USA and UK all use 15ml tablespoons. Australian tablespoons measure 20ml. All cup and spoon measurements are level.

Measuring equipment
The difference between one country's measuring cups and another's is, at most, within a 2 or 3 teaspoon variance. (For the record, 1 Australian metric measuring cup holds approximately 250ml.)
The most accurate way of measuring dry ingredients is to weigh them. For liquids, use a clear glass or plastic jug having metric markings.

How to measure
When using graduated measuring cups, shake dry ingredients loosely into the appropriate cup. Do not tap the cup on a bench or tightly pack the ingredients unless directed to do so. Level the top of measuring cups and measuring spoons with a knife. When measuring liquids, place a clear glass or plastic jug having metric markings on a flat surface to check accuracy at eye level.

Dry measures

metric	imperial
15g	1/2oz
30g	1oz
60g	2oz
90g	3oz
125g	4oz (¼lb)
155g	5oz
185g	6oz
220g	7oz
250g	8oz (½lb)
280g	9oz
315g	10oz
345g	11oz
375g	12oz (¾lb)
410g	13oz
440g	14oz
470g	15oz
500g	16oz (1lb)
750g	24oz (1½lb)
1kg	32oz (2lb)

We use large eggs having an average weight of 60g.

Liquid measures

metric	imperial
30 ml	1 fluid oz
60 ml	2 fluid oz
100 ml	3 fluid oz
125 ml	4 fluid oz
150 ml	5 fluid oz (¼ pint/1 gill)
190 ml	6 fluid oz
250 ml (1cup)	8 fluid oz
300 ml	10 fluid oz (½ pint)
500 ml	16 fluid oz
600 ml	20 fluid oz (1 pint)
1000 ml (1litre)	1¾ pints

Helpful measures

metric	imperial
3mm	⅛in
6mm	¼in
1cm	½in
2cm	¾in
2.5cm	1in
6cm	2½in
8cm	3in
20cm	8in
23cm	9in
25cm	10in
30cm	12in (1ft)

Oven temperatures
These oven temperatures are only a guide. Always check the manufacturer's manual.

	°C (Celsius)	°F (Fahrenheit)	Gas Mark
Very slow	120	250	1
Slow	150	300	2
Moderately slow	160	325	3
Moderate	180 –190	350 – 375	4
Moderately hot	200 – 210	400 – 425	5
Hot	220 – 230	450 – 475	6
Very hot	240 – 250	500 – 525	7

at your fingertips

These elegant slipcovers store up to 10 mini books and make the books instantly accessible.

And the metric measuring cups and spoons make following our recipes a piece of cake.

Book Holder
Australia and overseas:
$8.95 (incl. GST).

Metric Measuring Set
Australia: $6.50 (incl. GST).
New Zealand: $A8.00.
Elsewhere: $A9.95.
Prices include postage and handling. This offer is available in all countries.

Mail or fax Photocopy and complete the coupon below and post to
ACP Books Reader Offer,
ACP Publishing, GPO Box 4967,
Sydney NSW 2001, or fax to (02) 9267 4967.

Phone Have your credit card details ready, then phone 136 116 (Mon-Fri, 8.00am-6.00pm; Sat, 8.00am-6.00pm).

Australian residents We accept the credit cards listed on the coupon, money orders and cheques.

Overseas residents We accept the credit cards listed on the coupon, drafts in $A drawn on an Australian bank, and also British, New Zealand and U.S. cheques in the currency of the country of issue. Credit card charges are at the exchange rate current at the time of payment.

Photocopy and complete coupon below

□ **Book Holder** □ **Metric Measuring Set**
Please indicate number(s) required.

Mr/Mrs/Ms _____

Address _____

_____

Postcode _____ Country _____

Ph: Business hours ( ) _____

I enclose my cheque/money order for $ _____ payable to ACP Publishing.

OR: please charge $ _____ to my □ Bankcard □ Mastercard

□ Visa □ American Express □ Diners Club

Expiry date ____ /____

| | | | | | | | | | | | | | | | |

Card number

Cardholder's signature _____

Please allow up to 30 days delivery within Australia.
Allow up to 6 weeks for overseas deliveries.
Both offers expire 31/12/03. HLMFF03

Food director Pamela Clark
Food editor Louise Patniotis
Stylist Kate Brown
Photographer Stuart Scott
Home economist Jeanette Schembri

ACP BOOKS STAFF

Editorial director Susan Tomnay
Creative director Hieu Chi Nguyen
Senior editor Julie Collard
Designer Mary Keep
Publishing manager (sales) Jennifer McDonald
Publishing manager (rights & new titles) Jane Hazell
Brand manager Donna Gianniotis
Pre-press Harry Palmer
Production manager Carol Currie

Publisher Sue Wannan
Group publisher Jill Baker
Chief executive officer John Alexander

Produced by ACP Books, Sydney.

Printing by Dai Nippon Printing in Hong Kong

Published by ACP Publishing Pty Limited, 54 Park St, Sydney; GPO Box 4088, Sydney, NSW 1028. Ph: (02) 9282 8618
Fax: (02) 9267 9438.
acpbooks@acp.com.au
www.acpbooks.com.au

To order books phone 136 116.

Send recipe enquiries to
Recipeenquiries@acp.com.au

Australia Distributed by Network Services, GPO Box 4088, Sydney, NSW 1028.
Ph: (02) 9282 8777 Fax: (02) 9264 3278.

United Kingdom Distributed by Australian Consolidated Press (UK), Moulton Park Business Centre, Red House Road, Moulton Park, Northampton, NN3 6AQ. Ph: (01604) 497 531
Fax: (01604) 497 533 acpukltd@aol.com

Canada Distributed by Whitecap Books Ltd, 351 Lynn Ave, North Vancouver, BC, V7J 2C4
Ph: (604) 980 9852 Fax: (604) 980 8197
customerservice@whitecap.ca
www.whitecap.ca

New Zealand Distributed by Netlink Distribution Company, Level 4, 23 Hargreaves St, College Hill, Auckland 1, Ph: (9) 302 7616.

Clark, Pamela.
Fast Fish.

Includes index.
ISBN 1 86396 295 6

1. Cookery (fish). 2. Quick and easy cookery.
I. Title. II. Title: Fast Fish. III. Title: Australian Women's Weekly.

641.692

© ACP Publishing Pty Limited 2003
ABN 18 053 273 546

Cover: Pea flapjacks with smoked trout, page 28.
Cover stylist: Sarah O'Brien
Cover photographer: Ian Wallace
Back cover: at left, Niçoise salad, page at right, Pissaladière, page 12.

The publishers would like to thank Bison Homewares for props used in photography.